Well Said, Well Spoken

**CORWIN
PRESS**

The Corwin Press logo—a raven striding across an open book—represents the happy union of courage and learning. We are a professional-level publisher of books and journals for K–12 educators, and we are committed to creating and providing resources that embody these qualities. Corwin's motto is "Success for All Learners."

736 Quotable Quotes for Educators

Well

Said,

Well

Spoken

Robert D. Ramsey

CORWIN PRESS, INC.
A Sage Publications Company
Thousand Oaks, California

For information:

Corwin Press, Inc.
A Sage Publications Company
2455 Teller Road
CORWIN Thousand Oaks, California 91320
PRESS E-mail: order@corwinpress.com

Sage Publications Ltd.
6 Bonhill Street
London EC2A 4PU
United Kingdom

Sage Publications India Pvt. Ltd.
M-32 Market
Greater Kailash I
New Delhi 110 048 India

Printed in the United States of America

Library of Congress Cataloging-in-Publication Data

Well said, well spoken: 736 quotable quotes for educators/(compiled)
by Robert D. Ramsey.
    P. Cm.
ISBN 0-7619-7769-4 (cloth)
ISBN 0-7619-7770-8 (paper)
    1. Quotations, English. I. Title: 736 quotable quotes for educators.
II. Ramsey, Roberts, D.
    PN6081 .W383 2001
    082--dc21   00-012373

This book is printed on acid-free paper.

01 02 03 04 05 06 10 9 8 7 6 5 4 3 2

Acquisitions Editor:	Robb Clouse
Editorial Assistant:	Kylee Liegl
Production Editor:	Denise Santoyo
Editorial Assistant:	Kathryn Journey
Cover Designer:	Michael Dubowe
Typesetter:	Denyse Dunn

CONTENTS

About the Author   vi

Introduction   1

Acknowledgments   3

The Quotations   4

Other Resources You
Should Know About   162

ABOUT THE AUTHOR

*R*obert D. Ramsey, EdD, is a life-long educator with front-line experience as a teacher, counselor, curriculum coordinator, personnel director, associate superintendent, acting superintendent, and adjunct professor. He currently works full-time as a freelance writer in Minneapolis. He is the author of several successful books for parents and educators and a frequent contributor to numerous popular journals and newspapers.

Throughout his career as a leader of leaders in three award-winning school districts in two different states, Ramsey has been an avid collector of quips, quotes, and anecdotes that speak directly to today's principals and teachers. This current publication of the best from his collection just may be too good to pass up.

Other Books by Robert D. Ramsey

The Principals' Book of Lists

501 Tips for Teachers

Lead, Follow, or Get Out of the Way

Fiscal Fitness for School Administrators

INTRODUCTION

$\int$ ometimes, the best way to say something is to let someone else say it for you. This is especially true in a society obsessed with sound bites, when attention spans are short and a one-sentence sermon is about all most people ever get.

When every word has to count, educated people need ready access to a rich variety of quotes as a source of self-inspiration and to help get their point across to others. Principals and teachers need them more than most.

Well Said, Well Spoken is an upbeat, sassy compilation of classic, contemporary quotes and anecdotes for educators that features topics and sources not found in other references. Where else can you find the best thoughts of ordinary colleagues, the words of Sitting Bull, the Ayatollah Khomeini, a former drummer for the Grateful Dead, Mike Tyson, and rapper Ice T, along with the wisdom of Shakespeare, Lincoln, and Churchill, all in the same volume?

In addition to the usual respected scholars, statespersons, writers, politicians, and philosophers, this collection includes quotes from real teachers and administrators, regular students like those you work with every day, sports figures, rockers, rappers, bottom-line business leaders, and others representing all walks of life. Whoever said that insight, wisdom, and humor are limited to the ancient, the famous, the learned, or the high and mighty?

This one-of-a-kind collection is a user-friendly, fingertip resource packed with thought-provoking quotations that today's busy professionals can use as attention getters, point makers, openers, closers, and clinchers for all occasions. Best of all, it showcases only topics that educators think about, worry about, and talk about every day!

The *Well Said, Well Spoken* collection is different because

- It is comprehensive: Over 700 quotations on more than 160 subjects that principals and teachers care about most.

- It is current: These quotes are not just about the same, tired old standards—time-tested favorites are included, but many selections are as timely as this morning's headlines (it's not just dead folks who have something worthwhile to say).

- It is cutting edge: Many references included are traditional—this doesn't mean stuffy—whereas others are admittedly new age and provocative.

- It is *just* for principals and teachers: The collection isn't intended for the general public; it is limited to subjects of interest to today's educators.

As an educator, if you have room on your bookshelf for only one collection of quotations, *Well Said, Well Spoken* may be just what you are looking for. For many principals and teachers on the firing line today, the *Well Said, Well Spoken* collection, developed specifically for "school people," is the best choice available.

ACKNOWLEDGMENTS

Every item in this collection has been contributed by others—the living, the dead, the famous, the not-so-famous, and even the anonymous. I can't acknowledge them all personally, but I must acknowledge three special people:

> Robb Clouse, who understands that a good editor is more encourager than critic

> Joyce Ramsey, who turns scribbles into a printable product

> Marie White, who generously shared her personal collection of quotations

Without their contributions, this book would still be an idea waiting to happen. Thanks for helping breathe life into my vision.

Robert D. Ramsey

ABILITY

Ability may get you to the top, but it takes character to keep you there.

—John Wooden

There is something that is much more scarce, something rarer than ability. It is the ability to recognize ability.

— Robert Half

Do what you can, with what you have, where you are.

—Teddy Roosevelt

Ability is the act of getting credit for all the home runs that somebody else hits.

—Casey Stengel

ADVERTISING

Advertising is the rattling of a stick in a swill bucket.
—George Orwell

You can tell the ideals of a nation by its advertisements.
—Norman Douglas

Advertising can be described as the science of arresting the human intelligence long enough to get money from it.
—Stephen Leacock

Advertising is legalized lying.
—H. G. Wells

ADVICE

Don't be troubled if the temptation to give advice is irresistible; the ability to ignore it is universal.
—Anonymous

Wise men don't need advice. Fools won't take it.

—Benjamin Franklin

———•———

See everything. Overlook a great deal. Improve a little.

—Pope John XXIII

———•———

Work like you don't need money, love like you've never been
hurt, and dance like no one's watching.

—Ray Denning

———•———

Kisses aren't contracts and presents aren't promises. . . .
And even sunshine burns if you get too much. So plant your
own garden and nourish your own soul, instead of
waiting for someone to buy you flowers.

—Anonymous

———•———

Never play cards with a man called Doc. Never eat in a place
called Mom's. Never sleep with a woman
whose troubles are worse than your own.

—Nelson Algren

———•———

Never make excuses, never let them see you bleed, and never get separated from your baggage.
—Wesley Price,
"Three Rules of Professional Comportment for Writers"
The Writer's Quotation Book

———•———

There are 3 things we must do every day—
1) Get up. 2) Exercise. 3) Learn.
—Dr. Jim Benson

———•———

Never be more than you are.
—Steven Spielberg

———•———

Take it easy, go with the flow, and be nice to everybody.
—Coby Bell,
TV actor

———•———

Take it easy, but take it.
—Woody Guthrie

———•———

Live well, love much, laugh often.
—Slogan of the OASIS Restaurant,
Austin, TX

———•———

Learn some and think some and draw and paint and sing and dance and play and work every day some.

—Robert Fulghum

AIDS

AIDS poses its own threat to mankind, but unlike war, it is a battle from within, knowing no borders or national boundaries.

—Elisabeth Kubler-Ross, M.D.

Misinformation about AIDS is more contagious than the disease itself.

—Gavin de Becker

ALCOHOL

When you stop drinking, you have to deal with that marvelous personality that started you drinking in the first place.

—Jimmy Breslin

An alcoholic spends his life committing
suicide on the installment plan.

—Laurence J. Peter

We are dealing with alcohol—
cunning, baffling, and powerful.

— AA Saying

The disease is called alcohol-ism, not alcohol-wasm.

—Terrence Gorski

But suicide, quick or slow, a sudden spill or a gradual oozing
away through the years, is the price John Barleycorn exacts. No
friend of his ever escapes making the just, due payment.

—Jack London

AMBITION

Keep away from people who belittle your ambitions.
Small people always do that, but the really great
make you feel that you, too, can become great.

—Mark Twain

*Keeping up with the Joneses was a full-time job with my
mother and father. It was not until many years later . . .
that I realized how much cheaper it was to
drag the Joneses down to my level.*

—Quentin Crisp

———

AMERICA

*Double—no triple—our troubles and we'd still be
better off than any other people on earth.*

—Ronald Reagan

———

*The only position in America more important
than president is citizen.*

—Jimmy Carter

———

*Ours is the only country deliberately
founded on a good idea.*

—John Gunther

———

*America is the only nation that proclaims the
"pursuit of happiness" as a national goal.*

—Walter Mondale

———

America is the only country without a line of people waiting—wanting to get out.

—Michael Greene

———•———

In the United States, there is more space where nobody is than where anybody is. That is what makes America what it is.

—Gertrude Stein

———•———

ART

There is nothing new in art except talent.

—Anton Chekov

———•———

Art is not a thing; it is a way.

—*Elbert Hubbard*

———•———

ATTENDANCE

If you don't come to class, you don't get to pass.

—Old Teacher Saying

———•———

Those who are absent are always wrong.

—*English Proverb*

———•———

BABIES

Babies are such a nice way to start people.
— Don Herold

There is no finer investment for any community than putting milk in babies.
—Winston Churchill

All babies look like Winston Churchill.
—Edward R. Murrow

BOOKS

Literature and butterflies are the two sweetest passions known to man.
—Vladimir Nabokov

*There is more treasure in books than in all
the pirates' loot on Treasure Island.*
—Walt Disney

———•———

*The man who does not read good books has no
advantage over the man who can't read them.*
—Mark Twain

———•———

*When you sell a man a book, you don't sell him 12 ounces of
paper and ink and glue—you sell him a whole new life.*
—Christopher Morley

———•———

Make your books your companions.
—The Talmud

———•———

We can have too many bombs but not too many books.
—Mary Ann Grossman

———•———

Americans like fat books and thin women.
—Russell Baker

———•———

*There are no bad books, any more than
there are no ugly women.*
—Anatole France

———•———

Never loan books, for no one ever returns them; the only books I have in my library are books that other folks have lent me.

—Anatole France

* * *

A book is the only place in which you can examine a fragile thought without breaking it, or explore an explosive idea without fear it will go off in your face.

—Edward G. Morgan

* * *

No one is going to curl up at the beach with a computer.

—Jonathon Lazear

* * *

This will never be a civilized country until we expend more money on books than we do for chewing gum.

—Elbert Hubbard

* * *

BOSSES

By working faithfully eight hours a day, you may eventually get to be a boss and work twelve hours a day.

—Robert Frost

* * *

*W*hen your boss is mad, wait until he's in the right mood.
Never approach fire with gas.

—Rick Mickenberg,
Taxi Driver Wisdom

———•———

*T*he boss isn't always right;
but the boss is always the boss.

—Anonymous

———•———

*N*o bosses is better than money.

—William Least Heat Moon

———•———

*T*he boss drives his people; the leader coaches his.
The boss uses authority; the leader wins goodwill.
The boss keeps them guessing; the leader arouses their enthusiasm.
The boss talks about "I," the leader makes it "we."
The boss makes work drudgery; the leader makes work a game.
The boss says "Go"; the leader says "Let's go."

—Ted Pollock

———•———

I want employees who will show me the possibilities. . . .The
goal of the gifted boss is to be worthy of exceptional talent.

—Dale Dauten

———•———

BUDGETS

The budget is a mythical bean bag.

—Will Rogers

The only good budget is a balanced budget.

—Adam Smith

BUREAUCRACY

Bureaucracy is a giant mechanism operated by pygmies.

—Honoré de Balzac

*Bureaucracy defends the status quo long past
the time when the quo has lost its status.*

—Laurence J. Peter

Guidelines for Bureaucrats:
1. *When in charge, ponder;*
2. *When in trouble, delegate; and*
3. *When in doubt, mumble.*

—James H. Bowen

A bureaucrat's idea of cleaning up his files is to make a copy of every paper before he destroys it.

—Laurence J. Peter

———•———

I learned from the army it's easier to tell the people in the offices what they want to hear because if you don't there's always someone higher up who wants you to fill out a longer form.

—Frank McCourt

———•———

C

CENSORSHIP

To limit the press is to insult a nation; to prohibit reading of certain books is to declare the inhabitants to be either fools or slaves.
—Claude Helvetius

The ultimate censorship is the flick of the dial.
—Tom Smothers

CHANGE

The only person who loves a change is a wet baby.
—Ray Blitzer

We must change in order to survive.
—Pearl Bailey

*P*robably the most dramatic metaphor for change as the watchword of our time is the experience of Russian Cosmonaut Krikaler who left Leningrad for a 313 day journey in space in 1991. Almost a year later, he returned to a city no longer on the map and a country that no longer existed.

—Anonymous

*P*eople don't change that much. Don't waste time trying to put in what was left out. Try to draw out what was left in.

—Marcus Buckingham

*A*ll great changes are irksome to the human mind.

—John Adams

*Y*ou can't step into the same river twice.

—Herculeitus

*W*ho gives a man permission to change? *H*e gives it to himself.

—Gail Sheehy

CHARITY

The Lord loveth a cheerful giver.
He also accepts from a grouch.
                                    —Red O'Donnell

———•———

In charity, there are no excesses.
                                    —Francis Bacon

———•———

CHARTER SCHOOLS

Critics and advocates alike are watching closely
to see whether the movement [charter schools] leads
to more than a small set of "boutique" schools
that cannot be replicated elsewhere.
                                    —Kyo Yamashiro
                                    and Lisa Carlos

———•———

The charter idea does not guarantee that every school
is going to be a good school. The idea is that we're better off
allowing people to carry out their dreams as long as
they're held accountable for the results.
                                    —Joe Nathan

———•———

*O*ur school runs more like a
community center than a school.
—Myong Pak, Principal,
K-4 Charter School

CHEATING

*H*e is most cheated who cheats himself.
—Leonard Drozd

---

*C*lass, who can tell me what I have preserved in this jar?
No, it's not a pig or a baby cow . . . it's the last student
who got caught cheating on one of my tests.
—Glasbergen *cartoon caption*

---

*O*ne year, two guys each had a solid A going into the
final chemistry exam. They were so confident that the weekend
before finals, they decided to go out of town to party with
friends. Because of bad hangovers, they overslept and
didn't make it back until Monday morning.

Rather than taking the final then, they explained to the professor
that they had planned to come back in time to study, but they
had a flat tire without a spare, so they didn't get back in time.

The professor agreed that they could make up the final on the following day. The next day, the professor placed them in separate rooms, handed them a test booklet and told them to begin. They looked at the first problem that was worth five points.

"Cool," each of them thought. "This is going to be easy." They did that problem and turned the page. They were unprepared, however, for what they saw on the next page. It said: "Which tire? Ninety-five points."

—Story told by
Harvey MacKay

CHILDREN

Let us put our minds together and see what life we can make for our children.

—Tatenka Iyotak (Sitting Bull)

If America hopes to secure its future, children must come first.

—Ernest L. Boyer

I really believe that children do spell love "t-i-m-e" and
if you don't give them time, they're going to sense
the feeling of alienation and rejection.

—Rev. Che Ahn

⸻ ⸻

*S*o long as little children are allowed to suffer,
there is no true love in this world.

—Isadora Duncan

⸻ ⸻

*E*very child is a unique human being who grows at
his or her individual rate—except in schools.

—Jim Grant

⸻ ⸻

*L*eave no child behind.

—Goal of the
Children's Defense Fund

⸻ ⸻

*W*e must all work to make the world worthy of its children.

—Pablo Casals

⸻ ⸻

*K*ids, like cats, need time to purr.

—Fred T. Wilhelms

⸻ ⸻

If you want to see what children can do,
you must stop giving them things.

—Norman Douglas

———•———

Children are the living messages we send
to a time we will not see.

—Neil Postman

———•———

Children can catch fear and hatred from people around them
more quickly than they catch measles.

—Norman Vincent Peale

———•———

What the best and wisest parent wants for his own child,
that must the community want for all its children.

—John Dewey

———•———

So often we wallow in our children's problems
rather than exult in their strengths and possibilities.

—Marian Wright Edelman

———•———

The only time the average child is good as gold is on April 15.

—Ivern Boyett

———•———

*C*hildren are unpredictable. You never know what
inconsistency they're going to catch you in next.

—Franklin P. Jones

———

*C*hildren need love, especially when they do not deserve it.

—Harold S. Hulbert

———

*A*t every step, the child should be allowed to meet
the real experience of life; the thorns should never
be plucked from the roses.

—Ellen Kay

———

*A*ll people must be protectors of all children.

—Don Shelby,
TV anchorman

———

*E*veryone needs to hear from kids.

—Ashley Tomosen,
high school sophomore

———

*I*t's one thing to be in touch with your inner child, but when
your inner child is actually driving the car, you're in trouble.

—Gail Sheehy

———

COLLEGE

A man who has never gone to school may steal a freight car;
but if he has a university education,
he may steal the whole railroad.

—Teddy Roosevelt

The things taught in schools and colleges are not an
education, but the means of education.

—Ralph Waldo Emerson

A professor is one who talks in someone else's sleep.

—W. H. Auden

COMMITTEES

What is a committee? A group of the unwilling,
picked from the unfit, to do the unnecessary.

—Richard Harkness

If Columbus had an advisory committee he
would probably still be at the dock.

—Justice Arthur Goldberg

*A committee takes hours to put into minutes
what can be done in seconds.*

—Judy Castring

———•———

*Committee work is like a soft chair—
easy to get into but hard to get out of.*

—"Wit & Humor,"
Supervision *magazine*

———•———

*You'll find in no park or city a monument
to a committee.*

—Victoria Pasternak

———•———

A committee of one gets things done.

—Joe Ryan

———•———

COMPUTERS

*Who's looking to break into your computer? At least,
so far, the prowler is more likely to be a bored
tech-savvy teenager than a master thief.*

—Steve Gibson

———•———

Man is still the most extraordinary computer of all.

—John F. Kennedy

———

*If the automobile had followed the same development
as the computer, a Rolls Royce would today cost $100,
get a million miles per gallon and explode
once a year killing everyone inside.*

—Robert Cringely

———

The computer is a moron.

—Peter Drucker

———

Computers, like elephants, never forget.

—Richard Smith

———

*The real danger is not that computers will begin to think like
man, but that man will begin to think like computers.*

—Sydney J. Harris

———

CONSULTANTS

*Consultants look at your watch, tell you
the time and send you a bill.*

—Old Joke
(source unknown)

———•———

*An expert is a man who doesn't know all the answers, but is
sure that if he is given enough money he can find them.*

—R. Fletcher

———•———

*My greatest strength as a consultant
is to be ignorant and ask a few questions.*

—Peter Drucker

———•———

*A consultant is someone who believes
that the best things in life are fees.*

—"Wit & Wisdom"
Supervision *magazine*

———•———

CRIME

Crime is contagious.

—Justice Louis D. Brandeis

———

Crime expands according to our willingness to put up with it.

—Barry Forbes

———

Juvenile delinquency starts in the high chair
and ends in the death chair.

—James D. C. Murray

———

The chief problem in any community cursed with crime
is not the punishment of the criminal, but the preventing
of the young from being trained to crime.

—W. E. B. Du Bois

———

Poverty is the mother of crime.

—Marcus Aurelius

———

The whole reason for juvenile delinquency
is mental unemployment.

—Jackie Gleason

———

DEATH

Death twitches my ear, "Live," he says, "I am coming."
—*Virgil*

———◆———

Fear of death is worse than death itself.
—*Proverb*

———◆———

*I'm not afraid to die, I just don't want to
be there when it happens.*
—*Woody Allen*

———◆———

To die is landing on some distant shore.
—*John Dryden*

———◆———

DEMOCRACY

Democracy is the art of thinking independently together.
—Alexander Meiklejohn

———

Democracy is the recurrent suspicion that more than half of the people are right more than half of the time.
—E. B. White

———

Freedom is nothing else but a chance to be better.
—Albert Camus

———

Eternal vigilance is the price of liberty.
—Wendell Phillips

———

DISCIPLINE

Punish the incident and treat the problem.
—Anonymous

———

In the judicial, social and educational circumstances in which we live, we must not . . . endanger the physical and mental well-being of a minor with any type of corporal punishment.

—Dorit Beinisch,
Israel Supreme Court Justice

———•———

It is true that many of the causes of discipline problems lie within the nature of our society as well as within the nature of our schools.

—Eugene R. Howard

———•———

DREAMS

*Dreams are like letters from God.
Isn't it time you answered your mail?*

—Marie Louise von Franz

———•———

Sometimes, dreams are wiser than waking.

—William Least Heat-Moon

———•———

If you dream it, you can make it so.

—Belva Davis

———•———

A #2 pencil and a dream can take you anywhere.
—Joyce Myers

When we can't dream any longer we die.
—Emma Goldman

DRUGS

Drugs will kick your butt every time.
—Former L. A. prostitute

*It's not okay to push or use drugs
even if every person in America is doing it.*
—Marian Wright Edelman

The best time not to do drugs or alcohol is the first time.
—Mickey Mantle

Chemical use is not a right of passage.
—Pam Canning,
Prevention Specialist

*C*ocaine isn't habit-forming. I should know—
I've been using it for years.
—Tallulah Bankhead

*W*hen the drug trip or alcohol binge is over,
the problems will have remained the same
or gotten worse.
—Recovering 16-year-old

EATING DISORDERS

It is now fashionable to be thin, but if it were fashionable to be fat, women would force-feed themselves like geese.

—Una Stannard

———•———

Anorexia is a way to feel you control one thing in your life—eating.
When you have anorexia, you feel like you're the fattest cow who ever lived.

—Dawn Langstroth,
recovering anorexic

———•———

A street peddler was telling a friend about how tough things had gotten. To cut costs, he had begun to feed his horses fewer oats each day. For a while, things were looking up.

"Then," he lamented, "just when I had the horse trained
to eat nothing at all—he died!"

—Internet story
(source unknown)

The worship of the willowy super model has become a cult.

—William Jeffocoate, M.D.

EDUCATION

*Educated men are as much superior to
uneducated men as the living are to the dead.*

—Aristotle

---

*Training is everything . . . cauliflower is
nothing but cabbage with a college education.*

—Mark Twain

Civilization is a race between education and catastrophe.

—H. G. Wells

Education is not the filling of a pail, but the lighting of a fire.
—W. B. Yeats

———————

The secret of education is respect for the pupil.
—Ralph Waldo Emerson

———————

*We are not at a point where we must educate our children in
what no one knew yesterday, and prepare
our schools for what no one knows yet.*
—Margaret Mead

———————

*Education makes a people easy to lead, but difficult to drive;
easy to govern, but impossible to enslave.*
—Lord Brougham

———————

ENTHUSIASM

Nothing great was ever achieved without enthusiasm.
—Ralph Waldo Emerson

———————

*There is a name for people who are
not excited about their work—unemployed.*
—God's Little Devotional Book

———————

ENVIRONMENT

We won't have a society if we destroy the environment.
—Margaret Mead

*Man is messy; but any creature that can
create space vehicles can probably cope.*
—George F. Will

*Man is a complex being: he makes
deserts bloom—and lakes die.*
—Gil Stern

We are locked into a system of fouling our own nest.
—Garvett Hardin

Things are not as bad as they seem. They are worse.
—Bill Press

EXCELLENCE

The power of excellence is overwhelming.
—Gen. "Chappie" James

Don't settle for excellence. Strive for greatness.

—Anonymous

———•———

We are what we repeatedly do. Excellence, therefore, is not an act, but a habit.

—Aristotle

———•———

Excellence is an attitude.

—Richard Capen, Jr.

———•———

Excellence is more fun than mediocrity.

—Len Berry, M.D.

———•———

EXERCISE

If you ruin your body, where will you live?

—Anonymous

———•———

*E*xercise. Exercise. Exercise. It remains the single most potent
anti-aging medication known to humankind.
—Gail Sheehy

———•———

*I*f I had my way I'd make health catching, instead of disease.
—Robert G. Ingersoll

———•———

I'm in great shape—every artery's hard as a rock.
—Joe E. Lewis

———•———

*W*hen I feel like exercise, I lie down until the feeling passes.
—Robert M. Hutchins

———•———

*O*besity is really widespread.
—Joseph Kern II

———•———

I get my exercise acting as a pallbearer
to my friends who exercise.
—Chauncey Depew

———•———

*Exercise is bunk. If you are healthy, you don't need it;
if you are sick, you shouldn't take it.*

—Henry Ford

EXPECTATIONS

*The incredible power of a teacher comes from
modeling high expectations.*

—Larry Bell

Expectations are everything.

—Dale Dauten

---

*Nothing is more important than what you expect. . . .
If you expect too little, you rob yourself.*

—Dr. Robert Schuller

EXPERIENCE

*We learn from experience. A man never wakes up
his second baby just to see it smile.*

—Grace Williams

---

*E*xperience is knowledge of what used to work.

—*Anonymous*

———•———

*G*ood judgment comes from experience,
and experience comes from bad judgment.

—*Barry LePatner*

———•———

F

FACTS

Get your facts first, and then you can distort them as much as you please.

—Mark Twain

———

There are no eternal facts as there are no absolute truths.

—Friedrich Nietzsche

———

Facts do not cease to exist just because they are ignored.

—Aldous Huxley

———

FAILURE

A setback only paves the way for a comeback.

—Evander Holyfield

———

*E*very man's got to figure to get beat sometime.

—Joe Louis

———•———

*E*ver tried? Ever failed? No matter.
Try again. Fail again. Fail better.

—Samuel Beckett

———•———

*F*ailure is not the falling down, but the staying down.

—Mary Pickford

———•———

*F*ailure is an event—not a person.

—Zig Ziglar

———•———

*T*o err is human, but when the eraser wears out
ahead of the pencil, you're overdoing it.

—J. Jenkins

———•———

FAME

*F*ame is a vapor, popularity is an accident,
riches take wings. Only one thing endures—character.

—Horace Greeley

———•———

*The day will come when everyone will be
famous for fifteen minutes.*

—Andy Warhol

FAMILY

*Growing up in a loving home is the
best break anyone can have.*

—Walter Mondale

*There are no illegitimate children—
only illegitimate parents.*

—Judge Leon Yankwich

*What is done by the family in the home environment
has far greater influence on children than
anything a school can do or undo.*

—Terrell H. Bell,
U.S. Commissioner of Education

The family is the nucleus of civilization.

—Will Durant

FASHION

Beauty comes in all sizes—not just size 5.

—Roseanne

———•———

Dress for the job you want rather than the one you have.

—Sue Morem

———•———

I base my fashion taste on what doesn't itch.

—Gilda Radner

———•———

Blue jeans are the greatest invention since the gondola.

—Diane Vreeland,
Vogue *editor*

———•———

FAX MACHINES

*What did the person who owned the
first FAX machine do with it?*

—"Wit & Humor,"
Supervision *magazine*

———•———

FRIENDSHIP

A friend is a gift you give yourself.
—Robert Louis Stevenson

———•———

*The man with a host of friends who slaps on the back every-
body he meets is regarded as the friend of nobody.*
—Aristotle

———•———

*One friend in a lifetime is much; two are many;
three are hardly possible.*
—Henry Brooks Adams

———•———

First of all, you have to be your own best friend.
—Christine Grimaldi

———•———

"He is my friend" is a powerful statement.
—Jimmy Carter

———•———

A friend is one who knows all about you and likes you anyway.
—Christi Warner

———•———

*Y*ou can make more friends in two months by becoming
interested in other people than you can in two years
by trying to get them interested in you.

—*Dale Carnegie*

———•———

FUNDAMENTALS

*T*he minute you get away from fundamentals—
whether it's proper technique, work ethic, or
mental preparation—the bottom can fall out of your game,
your school work, your job, whatever you're doing.

—*Michael Jordan*

———•———

FUTURE

*A*in't no future in the past.

—*Anonymous*

———•———

*T*he future is not some place we are going,
but one we are creating.

—*John Schaar*

———•———

Tomorrow is always the busiest day of the week.

—Jonathon Lazear

———•———

*The future belongs to those who believe in
the beauty of their dreams.*

—Eleanor Roosevelt

———•———

*America's future walks through the
doors of our schools every day.*

—Mary Jean LeTendre

———•———

The handwriting on the wall may be a forgery.

—Ralph Hodgson

———•———

GANGS

Gangs are everywhere.
They are the catchall of throwaway kids.

—Anonymous

Gangs are only as strong as the
community allows them to be.

—Unidentified
police liaison officer

GEEKS

Geeks are people who become so engrossed in a particular
field or skill that the rest of their appearance and life becomes
out of balance, usually to a humorous effect.

Geeks know they're geeks and are proud of it. Nerds don't know they are nerds.

—Robert Stevens,
Chief Inspector,
Geek Squad, Inc.

Bill Gates used to be a geek. Now he's just a businessman with a bad haircut.

—John Keller

GIFTED

A child prodigy is a youngster who is too young to be as old as he is.

—Even Esar

Everyone is a genius at least once a year; a real genius has his original ideas closer together.

—C. C. Lichtenberg

Talent is what you possess; genius is what possesses you.

—Malcolm Cowley

GOALS

What keeps me going is goals.
—Muhammed Ali

Goal setting is the strongest force for human motivation.
—Don Clark

Short-term goals are refueling stations along the journey.
—Scott A. Romeo

*Obstacles are those frightful things you see
when you take your eyes off your goals.*
—Henry Ford

GOSSIP

Gossip is mischievous.
—Hesiod

Whoever gossips to you will gossip about you.
—Spanish Proverb

*It is the gossip columnist's business to write about
what is none of his business.*

—Louis Kronenberger

———•———

Throw dirt enough, and some will stick.

—Proverb

———•———

GOVERNMENT

That government is best which governs the least.

—Thomas Jefferson

———•———

*The country has come to feel the same when Congress
is in session as when the baby gets hold of a hammer.*

—Will Rogers

———•———

*Government is too big and important
to be left to the politicians.*

—Chester Bowler

———•———

There is no right government except good government.

—George Santayana

———•———

Every nation has the government it deserves.

—Joseph Marie Maistre

GRADES

The world is run by C students.

—*Anonymous*

*I'm getting dumber every day, and it's all too embarrassing.
. . . I'm the only kid in the history of education
with a straight "Z" average.*

—*"Peppermint Patty"*
(*"Peanuts" comic strip character created by Charles Schulz*)

Inside every C+ student is a B– student trying to get out.

—Art Peterson

GRAFFITI

A white wall is the fool's paper.

—*French Proverb*

Graffiti—memorable art too good to be published.
—Edmund H. Volkart

———•———

GUNS

What in the name of conscience will it take to pass a truly effective gun-control law? Now in the hour of tragedy, let us spell out our grief in constructive action.
—Lyndon B. Johnson

———•———

Anyone pushing through anti-gun legislation is a bloody traitor.
—N. H. Stuart

———•———

The real gunslingers always tried to avoid pulling their guns.
—Michael Crichton

———•———

H

HABIT

*The chains of habit are too weak to be felt
until they are too strong to be broken.*
—Samuel Johnson

HAPPINESS

There are no Cliff Notes for happiness.
—Anonymous

Happiness is not a state to arrive at, but a manner of traveling.
—Margaret Lee Runbeck

HEADSTART

*What the founder of Headstart says is all too true—
every baby born in this country gets on one of two trains—
one bound for heaven or one bound for hell. And the
children on the train to hell see the kids on the other train.
The tragedy is that our society has built so few switching
stations to help youngsters change their lives.*

—Eli Newberger, M.D.

———•———

HEALTH EDUCATION

*We need to start with our literate society and convince
our policymakers of the importance of health education from
kindergarten to 12th grade. We have to teach
our children to be healthy.*

—Jocelyn Elders

———•———

HEREDITY

Heredity is nothing but stored environment.

—Luther Burbank

———•———

The environmentalists seem to believe that if cats gave birth to kittens in a stove, the offspring would be biscuits.

—Abraham Myerson

———

HISTORY

What history teaches us is that we have never learned anything from it.

—George Wilhelm Hegel

———

History is the science of man.

—José Ortega y Gasset

———

The study of history is the beginning of political wisdom.

—John Bodin

———

HOMEWORK

Why study? The more we know, the more we forget. The more we forget, the less we know. The less we know, the less we forget. The less we forget, the more we know. Why study?

—Milton Berle

———

Now I'm waiting for a law banning homework. I don't know why, but I have a feeling I'll be waiting a long time.

—Cindy Okrzesik,
7th grader

———•———

Homework is also a parent-teacher relationship tool.

—Renee Rosenblum-Lowden

———•———

HOPE

Hope is a risk that must be run.

—George Barnanas

———•———

There is no medicine like hope.

—O. S. Marden

———•———

If one truly lost hope, one would not be on hand to say so.

—Eric Bentley

———•———

HUMOR

Humor is the balance wheel of life.

—Ruth Bell Graham

———•———

Humor is like lettuce. In addition to being not particularly nourishing, jokes go bad soon after being brought to market.

—Collin Covert

———•———

I

IDEAS

Great ideas have a very short shelf life.

—John M. Shanahan

———

Ideas shape the course of history.

—John Maynard Keynes

———

INHERITANCE

You should leave your kids enough so that they can do anything, but not so much that they can do nothing.

—Warren Buffet

———

INTELLIGENCE

Everybody is ignorant, only on different subjects.

—Will Rogers

———

*E*ggheads, unite! You have nothing to lose but your yolks.

—Adlai Stevenson

———•———

*E*very child ought to be more intelligent than his parents.

—Clarence Darrow

———•———

*T*here are many kinds of intelligence. Language ability; math
ability; body-sense, like that of a dancer;
interpersonal skills and musical ability are all intelligence.

—Bruce Brandt,
math scholar

———•———

INTERNET

*T*he Internet is a great equalizer.

—Al Cooper

———•———

*T*he Internet will help achieve "friction-free capitalism."

—Bill Gates

———•———

KNOWLEDGE

*Knowledge without conscience
is the ruination of the soul.*

—François Rabelais

———•———

*Knowledge is like money. If you keep quiet about it,
people will think you've got more than you have.*

—Anonymous

———•———

What I don't know isn't knowledge.

—H. C. Beeching

———•———

We do not know one millionth
of one percent about anything.

—*Thomas Edison*

Beware of false knowledge;
it is more dangerous than ignorance.

—*George Bernard Shaw*

L

LANGUAGE

*E*nglish is a strange language. In English,
a fat chance and a slim chance mean the same thing.
—"Wit & Humor,"
Supervision *magazine*

---

*G*rammar is not a set of rules; it is something inherent
in the language, and language cannot exist without it.
It can be discovered, but not invented.
—Charlton Laird

---

*S*lang is a language that rolls up its sleeves,
spits on its hands and goes to work.
—Carl Sandburg

---

*S*lang is a poor man's poetry.
—John Moore

Latin's a dead language
As dead as dead can be;
It killed off all the Romans,
And now it's killing me.

           —Michael Kilgarriff

LAUGHTER

A good time to laugh is any time you can.

           —Linda Ellerbee

A good laugh is sunshine in the house.

           —William Makepeace Thackery

LAWYERS

Our courts have traded truth for process.

           —Mike Walz

It is better to be a mouse in a cat's mouth
than a man in a lawyer's hands.

—Spanish Proverb

Our court dockets are so crowded today it would be
better to refer to it as the "overdue process of law."

—Bill Vaughn

Whatever their other contributions to our society,
lawyers could be an important source of protein.

—Guindon cartoon caption

LEADERSHIP

An army of sheep led by a lion would defeat
an army of lions led by a sheep.

—Arab Proverb

It's not enough to be on the cutting edge. Now, you need to
be in the envelope of turbulence in front of the leading edge.

—Dr. Jim Benson

If you want to be a great leader, run ahead of a big parade.
—Anonymous

Being powerful is like being a lady.
If you have to tell people you are, you aren't.
—Margaret Thatcher

So much of what we call management
consists of making it difficult for people to work.
—Peter Drucker

The first responsibility of a leader is to define reality.
The last is to say thank-you.
—Max DePree

The best executive is the one who has sense enough to
pick good men to do what he wants done, and self-restraint
enough to keep from meddling while they do it.
—Teddy Roosevelt

A good supervisor is a catalyst, not a drill sergeant.
—Whitley David

You can't lead with an uncertain trumpet.
—G. Gordon Liddy

———•———

*The role of leaders is to turn lights on. We need to be the
most optimistic people in the organization.*
—Dr. Paul D. Houston

———•———

*Anyone can take a poll; but it takes
a true leader to move a nation.*
—Bob Dole

———•———

LEARNING

Somewhere, something incredible is waiting to be known.
—Carl Sagan

———•———

*In the world of the future, the new illiterate
will be the person who has not learned to learn.*
—Alvin Toffler

———•———

*In a knowledge-based economy,
the new coin of the realm is learning.*
—Robert Reich

———•———

The beautiful thing about learning is
nobody can take it away from you.

—B. B. King

———•———

The reasonable thing is to learn from those who can teach.

—Sophocles

———•———

Anyone who stops learning is old.

—Henry Ford

———•———

They know enough who know how to learn.

—Henry Brooks Adam

———•———

LIES

A lie can travel half way around the world
while the truth is putting on its shoes.

—Mark Twain

———•———

The biggest liar in the world is They Say.

—Douglas Malloch

———•———

We lie loudest who lie to ourselves.

—Eric Hoffer

———

A half-truth is a whole lie.

—Yiddish Proverb

———

LIFE

In spite of the high cost of living, it's still popular.

—from Retirement

———

Life is God's novel. Let Him write it.

—Isaac Bashevis Singer

———

*The first half of our lives is ruined by our parents;
and the second half by our children.*

—Clarence Darrow

———

*If people concentrated on the really important things of life,
there would be a shortage of fishing poles.*

—Doug Larson

———

Life is like a stone, skipping over clear water. You
don't know how many skips you're going to get, or for how long.
What's important are the ripples you make and
how they affect the ones around you.
—Donnie Christensen,
survivor of infection by a flesh-eating illness

———•———

Life's answers are within you.
—Richard A. Erickson, Ph.D.

———•———

No one gets out of the world alive, so the time to live,
learn, care, share, celebrate and love is now.
—Dr. Leo Buscaglia

———•———

Life is 10% what happens to me and 90% how I react to it.
—Lou Holtz

———•———

If you love life, life will love you back.
—A. Rubenstein

———•———

You only live once but if you work it right, once is enough.
—Joe E. Lewis

———•———

*Life can only be understood backwards
but it must be lived forward.*

—Sören Kierkegaard

Life is so daily.

—Anonymous

Whatever you do in life, 90% of it is half mental.

—Yogi Berra

Life isn't fair. It's a bummer, but it's true.

—Richard Carlson, Ph.D.

Life is too short to hide affection.

—Victor B. Miller

Life is too serious to be taken seriously.

—Anonymous

Life, it turns out, is not a struggle, it's a wiggle.

—John Rogers &
Peter McWilliams, Life 101

The purpose of life is a life of purpose.

—Robert Byrne

———•———

Life provides us with a teacher until we are wise enough to find our own.

—Charles Bates,
Pigs Eat Wolves

———•———

Life is what we make it, always has been, always will be.

—Grandma Moses

———•———

LISTENING

No one ever listened himself out of a job.

—Calvin Coolidge

———•———

It is impossible to overemphasize the immense need human beings have to be really listened to.

—Paul Tournier

———•———

A major portion of what we think we just heard is the product of our imagination.

Whoever listens most usually controls the situation.

—Veronique Vienne

* * *

When I ask you to listen to me
And you start giving advice
You have not done what I asked.
Listen! All I asked was that you listen.
Not talk or do—just hear me.
Advice is cheap: A quarter will get you both Dear
Abby and Billy Graham in the same newspaper.
And I can do for myself. I'm not helpless.
Maybe discouraged and faltering, but not helpless.

. . .

So please, listen and just hear me, and, if you want to talk,
Wait a minute for your turn; and I'll listen to you.

—Source unknown

* * *

LOVE

If falling in love is anything like learning to spell,
I don't want to do it. It takes too long.

—Glen, age 7

* * *

*T*ake away love and our earth is a tomb.

—Robert Browning

———•———

*L*ove cures people—both the ones who
give it and the ones who receive it.

—Karl Menninger

———•———

*S*pread love everywhere you go;
first of all, in your own house.

—Mother Teresa

———•———

*T*he story goes that a man was upset with his 3-year-old
daughter for wasting a roll of wrapping paper. Money was
tight and he became infuriated when the child tried to decorate
a box to put under the Christmas tree. Nevertheless, the little
girl brought the gift to her father and said,
"This is for you, Daddy."

He was embarrassed by his earlier overreaction, but his anger
flared again when he found the box was empty. He yelled
at her, "Don't you know that when you give a present
there's supposed to be something inside it?"

*The little girl looked up at him with tears in her eyes and said,
"Oh, Daddy, it's not empty. I blew kisses into the box.
All for you, Daddy."*

*The father was crushed. He put his arms around his little girl,
and he begged for forgiveness. It is told that the man kept that
box by his bed for years and whenever he was discouraged,
he would take out an imaginary kiss and remember
the love of the child who had put it there.*

—Anonymous from the Internet

In love there are no vacations.

—Marguerite Duras

LUCK

Luck never gives; it only lends.

—Swedish Proverb

Your luck is how you treat people.

—B. O'Donnell

The only thing that overcomes hard luck is hard work.

—Harry Golden

M

MARRIAGE

I married beneath me—all women do.
— Nancy Astor

———

Marriage is a mistake every man should make.
— George Jessel

———

Happiness in marriage is entirely a matter of choice.
— Jane Austin

———

Why does a woman work ten years to change a man's habits and then complain that he's not the man she married?
— Barbra Streisand

———

Marry in haste and repent in leisure.
— James Cabell

———

MATHEMATICS

Numbers constitute the only universal language.

—Nathaniel West

Let no one ignorant of mathematics enter here.

—Plato

MEDIA

Truth in journalism is usually found on the comic pages.

—Frank DeGennaro

*The news we receive through the media
is a proctological view of life.*

—Alan Cohen

Never argue with someone who buys ink by the barrel.

—Carl Holmstrom

News is the first draft of history.

—Ben Bradlee

The function of the press in society is to inform,
but the role is to make money.

—A. Liebling

———•———

The press, the movies, radio and television bear a
large share of the responsibility for the climate of fear . . .
which has enveloped the country and which
has become such a threat to our freedom.

—William T. Evjus

———•———

MEMORY

Memory is the thing you forget with.

—Alexander Chase

———•———

MONEY

The safest way to double your money is to
fold it over once and put it in your pocket.

—Kin Hubbard

———•———

Anyone who thinks there's safety in numbers
hasn't looked at the stock market pages.

—Irene Peter

———•———

Ever wonder if whoever invented the boomerang
also invented the credit card?

—Anonymous

———•———

Money is like manure. It does best if spread around.

—Thomas Fuller

———•———

Money costs too much.

—Ross MacDonald

———•———

MOTHERS

If everyone could have had my mother,
we wouldn't need a police force today.

—Adm. Thomas Moore

———•———

God could not be everywhere and
therefore He made mothers.

—Jewish Proverb

———•———

Simply having children does not make mothers.

—John A. Sheda

———•———

MOVIES

*What's the salvation of the movies? I say,
run 'em backwards. It can't hurt and it's worth a try.*

—Will Rogers

———•———

*The length of a film should be directly proportional
to the endurance of the human bladder.*

—Alfred Hitchcock

———•———

A wide screen just makes a bad movie twice as bad.

—Samuel Goldwyn

———•———

MUSIC

*Jazz will endure just as long as people hear it
through their feet instead of their brains.*

—John Philip Sousa

———•———

Without music, life would be a mistake.
　　　　　　　　　　　　　　—Friedrich Nietzsche

———•———

My music can make the blind see, the lame walk. . . .
It regenerates the ears, makes the liver quiver,
the bladder splatter and the knees freeze.
　　　　　　　　　　　　　　—Little Richard

———•———

Music can name the unnamable and
communicate the unknowable.
　　　　　　　　　　　　　　—Leonard Bernstein

———•———

No human culture has ever existed without music.
　　　　　　　　　　　　　　—Mickey Hart
　　　　　　　　　　　　(drummer, the Grateful Dead)

———•———

The man who disparages music as a luxury
and nonessential is doing the nation an injury.
　　　　　　　　　　　　　　—Woodrow Wilson

———•———

*A*ny tendency to consider music a luxury is dangerous. This patently false idea leads to devaluing music in general education, often to the point of eliminating it entirely when budgets are tight.

—Frederick Lieberman

*M*usic is no different than opium.

—Ayatollah Khomeini

*M*usic is the shorthand of emotion.

—Leo Tolstoy

N

NOTHING

*Nothing is often a good thing to do and
always a clever thing to say.*

—Anonymous

———•———

OPPORTUNITY

Opportunity is missed by most people because it is dressed in overalls and looks like work.

—Thomas Edison

A wise man will make more opportunities than he finds.

—Francis Bacon

PAPERWORK

What the world really needs is more love and less paperwork.
—Pearl Bailey

PARENTS

"Parent" is a verb.
—Richard G. Capen, Jr.

---

*Most of us become parents long before
we have stopped being children.*
—Mignon McLaughlin

In most cases I would say adults definitely need advice about raising children and the No. 1 place to look for it is probably sitting right on your couch with a bag of potato chips watching TV. That's right, your very own child.

—Brook Gessner,
15-year-old

If you had a point, what would it be?

—Teenager to parent

It is now possible for a child to have five parents: sperm donor, egg donor, the surrogate mother who carried the fetus and two adoptive parents.

—George Carlin

Deciding to have a child is to decide forever to have your heart walking around outside your body.

—Anonymous

God lends you your children until they're about 18. If you haven't made your point by then, it's too late.

—Betty Ford

Parents are allowed 20,000 mistakes
before they have to apply for a refill.

—Lawrence Kuiner

PEACE

The basic problems facing the world today
are not susceptible to a military solution.

—John F. Kennedy

In the future, no one wins a war . . .
there are degrees of loss, but no one wins.

—Brock Chisholm

War is only a cowardly escape from the problems of peace.

—Thomas Mann

The way to win an atomic war is to
make certain it never starts.

—Gen. Omar Bradley

In war, there are no unwounded soldiers.

—José Norosky

PEOPLE

There's a lot of human nature in people.
—Mark Twain

People have one thing in common, they are all different.
—Robert Zend

I've learned that you can tell a lot about a man by the way he handles three things: a rainy day; lost luggage; and tangled Christmas tree lights.
—Anonymous, age 52

Too bad that all the people who know how to run the country are busy driving taxi cabs or cutting hair.
—George Burns

PERFECTION

Good enough is better than perfect if it leaves time for fun.
—Judy Nollet

PERSEVERANCE

Talent takes you dancing, but perseverance buys your shoes.
—Michael Perry

———•———

PLAGIARISM

Artists . . . don't steal. But they do borrow without giving back.
—Ned Rorem

———•———

Taking something from one man and making it worse is plagiarism.
—George Moore

———•———

If you copy from one author, it's plagiarism. If you copy from two, it's research.
—Wilson Mizner

———•———

Adam was the only man who, when he said a good thing, knew that nobody had said it before him.
—Mark Twain

———•———

PLANNING

*H*ave a plan—and a Plan B.

—*Kirby Puckett*

———

*E*veryone has a plan until he gets hit.

—*Mike Tyson*

———

I always plan for the future. When the time comes,
if the plan is here and I'm not, it's no problem.
But if I'm here and the plan isn't, that's a problem.

—*Anonymous senior citizen*

———

*P*lan your work for today and every day,
then work your plan.

—*Norman Vincent Peale*

———

POETRY

A poem begins in delight and ends in wisdom.

—*Robert Frost*

———

I could no more define poetry than a terrier can define a rat.
—A. E. Houseman

———•———

There is no money in poetry;
but there's no poetry in money either.
—Robert Graves

———•———

POLICE

For the middle class, the police protect property,
give directions and help old ladies. For the urban poor,
the police are those who arrest you.
—Michael Harrington

———•———

Police are numbered in case they get lost.
—Spike Milligan

———•———

POLITICS

Politics is the gentle art of getting votes from the poor
and campaign funds from the rich.
—Oscar Ameringer

———•———

*P*olitics offers yesterday's answers to today's problems.
—Marshall McLuhan

*M*oney is the mother's milk of politics.
—Jesse Unruh

*A*ll politics is local.
—Tip O'Neill

PORNOGRAPHY

*P*ornography is an attempt to insult sex.
—D. H. Lawrence

I don't think pornography is very harmful,
but it is terribly, terribly boring.
—Noel Coward

*N*obody, including the Supreme Court,
knows what obscenity is.
—Norman Dorsen

POVERTY

The poor you always have with you.

—Jesus

———◆———

War on nations changes maps. War on poverty maps change.

—Muhammad Ali

———◆———

Wealth is conspicuous, but poverty hides.

—James Reston

———◆———

Every American baby has a 1 in 4 chance of being born in poverty here in the richest nation in the world. No other industrial nation allows its children to be the poorest part of their population.

—Marian Wright Edelman

———◆———

The worst country to be poor in is America.

—Arnold Toynbee

———◆———

*America is an enormous frosted cupcake
in the middle of millions of starving people.*

—Gloria Steinem

———◆———

If a free society cannot help the many who are poor,
it cannot save the few who are rich.

—John F. Kennedy

———•———

PRAISE

The applause of a single human being is of great consequence.

—Samuel Johnson

———•———

There is no praise to beat the sort you can put in your pocket.

—Moliére

———•———

PRAYER

Do not pray for easy lives. Pray to be stronger men.

—John F. Kennedy

———•———

Prayer is not an old woman's idle amusement . . .
it is the most potent instrument of action.

—Mohandas Gandhi

———•———

It is not well for a man to pray cream and live skim milk.
—Henry Ward Beecher

——◆——

PREJUDICE

It is never too late to give up your prejudices.
—Henry David Thoreau

——◆——

Prejudice is an opinion without judgment.
—Voltaire

——◆——

I am free of all prejudices. I hate everyone equally.
—W. C. Fields

——◆——

*The mind of the bigot is like the pupil of the eye;
the more light you pour upon it, the more it will contract.*
—Oliver Wendell Holmes, Jr.

——◆——

PREPARATION

I will prepare and someday my chance will come.
—Abraham Lincoln

——◆——

My favorite example of a man's need to be prepared
comes from the life of the great Houdini. . . . He made
the challenge that anyone, no matter how big they were,
could punch him in the stomach and he wouldn't
be hurt by it. He could take any punch.

One Halloween night . . . a young college student
came backstage and asked, "Is it true that
you can take any punch?"

Houdini said, "Yes."

Before Houdini had a chance to prepare himself,
the student gave him a quick jab. It was that
quick punch that killed the great Houdini.
He was rushed to the hospital,
but died the next day.

—John D. Gray, Ph.D.

———•———

PRINCIPALS

The most important person in the school is the principal.

—Hillary Clinton

———•———

Good principals make good teaching and learning possible.
—*from* 501 Ways to Boost Your Child's Success in School

———•———

Cabbie: "Mister, this is my first day driving a taxi. I don't know where the heck I'm going; but I'm going as fast as I can."

Passenger: "Now, there's a man who understands what it means to be a principal."
—The Mamchaks

———•———

Top 10 Reasons for Becoming a School Principal
10. *Lots of cool keys.*
9. *Choice of parking spots.*
8. *Hot lunch every day.*
7. *Free admission to games and concerts.*
6. *Neat office where you can read magazines and take naps.*
5. *Get to keep teachers after school.*
4. *Name often appears in print (usually graffiti).*
3. *Never grow old being around young people.*
2. *Chance to shape tomorrow today.*
1. *KIDS!!*
—*from* The Principals' Book of Lists

———•———

Headmasters (principals) have powers at their disposal which Prime Ministers have never yet been invested.
—Winston Churchill

You can have a bad school with a good principal; but you can't have a good school with a bad principal.
—Anonymous

Blessed are the administrators who do not have the answers to the problems of education and know enough to keep their mouths shut.
—Paul McClure

Those who can, do; those who can't, teach; and those who can do neither, administer.
—Collet Calverly

PRIORITIES

Keep the main thing the main thing.
—Carol Johnson

$\mathcal{G}$et your priorities straight. No one ever said on his death bed, "Gee, if I'd only spent more time at the office."

—H. Jackson Brown

PROBLEMS

$\mathcal{P}$roblems are only opportunities in work clothes.

—Henry J. Kaiser

$\mathcal{T}$hings go bad. They get better. Every job has its little problems. That's why they call them "jobs," not "summer camp."

—Harvey MacKay

$\mathcal{W}$ithout problems, there would be no possibility of triumph.

—Anonymous

$\mathcal{W}$hen confronted with a Goliath-sized problem, which way do you respond: "He's too big to hit," or like David, "He's too big to miss"?

—from God's Little Devotional Book

$\mathcal{A}$ problem well stated is a problem half solved.

—Charles F. Kettering

If there is no solution, there is no problem.

—*Anonymous*

———

Problems are messages.

—*Shakti Gawain*

———

No problem is so big and complicated
that it can't be run away from.

—*Charles Schulz,*
"Peanuts" comic strip

———

Every problem has in it the seeds of its own solution.

—*Norman Vincent Peale*

———

A problem is a chance for you to do your best.

—*Duke Ellington*

———

PROCRASTINATION

If you have to swallow a frog, don't look at it too long.
It won't get any prettier.

—*Zig Ziglar*

———

An hour of procrastination
is equivalent to an hour at the gym.
                    —Veronique Vienne

———•———

Vacillation and hesitation can become values too.
                    —Richard Capen, Jr.

———•———

Procrastination gives you something to look forward to.
                    —Joan Konner

———•———

PROGRESS

What we call "progress" is the exchange of
one nuisance for another nuisance.
                    —Havelock Ellis

———•———

Planned obsolescence is another name for progress.
                    —James Roche

———•———

PSYCHIATRY

*Anybody who goes to a psychiatrist
ought to have his head examined.*
—Samuel Goldwyn

———————

*Psychiatry is the art of teaching people how to
stand on their own feet while reclining on couches.*
—Shannon Fife

———————

*The diseases of the mind are more destructive
than those of the body.*
—Marcus Tullius Cicero

———————

PUBLICITY

What kills a skunk is the publicity it gives itself.
—Abraham Lincoln

———————

QUESTIONS

It's better to know some of the questions than all the answers.
—Leonard O. Pellicer

Once you have the questions right, the answers will come.
—The Celestine Prophecy

There are no embarrassing questions,
only embarrassing answers.
—Anonymous

QUOTATIONS

I quote others the better to express myself.
—Michael de Montaigne

I hate quotations.

—*Ralph Waldo Emerson*

———•———

A short saying oft contains much wisdom.

—*Sophocles*

———•———

RACISM

Racism is an adult disease.
Let's stop spreading it through children.

—Anonymous

———

Racism is man's greatest threat to man.

—Abraham Herchel

———

The plague of racism is insidious, entering our minds
as smoothly and quietly and invisibly as
airborne microbes enter our bodies.

—Maya Angelou

———

Being racist and sexist are a state of mind and a choice.

—Marian Wright Edelman

———

RELIGION

A small child was drawing a picture and his teacher said,
"That's an interesting picture. Tell me about it."

"It's a picture of God."

"But nobody knows what God looks like."

"They will when I get done."
—Internet story,
(source unknown)

———

*Y*ou were born God's original.
Try not to become someone's copy.
—Marian Wright Edelman

———

*G*od loves you just the way you are today,
but much too much to let you stay that way.
—Richard G. Capen, Jr.

———

*E*very time the puddle of human affairs is about to congeal,
the finger of God comes down to stir it.
—Arnold Toynbee

———

If you feel distant from God, who moved?

—Alan Cohen

———•———

If you are going the wrong direction, God allows U-turns.

—Anonymous

———•———

Why does God have a swear word for a name?

—Samuel Montgomery

———•———

God will forgive me, that's his business.

—Heinrich Heine

———•———

No one is useless to God.

—Max Lucado

———•———

God's fingerprint is on everything.

—Richard Carlson

———•———

God is the sum of all possibilities.

—Anonymous

———•———

All religions must be tolerated . . . for . . .
every man must go to heaven in his own way.
— Frederick the Great

I consider myself a Hindu, Christian,
Muslim, Jew, Buddhist and Confucian.
— Mohandus Gandhi

RESPONSIBILITY

The buck stops here.
— Harry S. Truman

A bad workman always blames his tools.
— Proverb

RETIREMENT

Good-bye tension. Hello pension.
— Retiring teacher

A wife's definition of retirement:
"Twice as much husband and half as much income."
—*from* Retirement

———————

There is a time for departure even when
there is no certain place to go.
—*Tennessee Williams*

———————

Retirement is just another word for
finally getting your priorities straight.
—Anonymous

———————

RISK TAKING

Sometimes you have to jump off the bridge
and build your wings on the way down.
—*Danielle Steele*

———————

When you bite the bullet, it may explode in your face.
—*Bob Dole*

———————

ROCK 'N' ROLL

The blues had a baby, and they called it rock 'n' roll.
—Muddy Waters

*When you're singing and playing rock 'n' roll,
you're on the leading edge of yourself.*
—Neil Young

*The effect of rock 'n' roll on young people is to turn them
into devil worshippers; to stimulate self-expression
through sex; to promote lawlessness.*
—Rev. Albert Carter

*If you are not careful, being a rock star
in today's world can kill you.*
—Mickey Hart
(former drummer, Grateful Dead)

*The turning point in the history of Western civilization
was reached with the invention of the electric guitar.*
—Lent Sinclair

ROLE MODELS

You have to be your own role model.
—Gen. Colin Powell

*Without heroes, we are all plain people
and don't know how far we can go.*
—Bernard Malamud

*We have few contemporary heroes, but we have plenty of
trash-talking, high-fiving, stuff-strutting celebrities who seem
transfixed by their own images. Is it any wonder that youngsters
disrespect authority? They've learned well from their "heroes"
who only watch out for number one.*
—Richard G. Capen, Jr.

*Whoever you are, there is someone younger
who thinks you are perfect.*
—Jacob Brande

Heroes seldom ask permission from the authorities.
—Sam Keen

The real heroes are noncelebrities.

—Ed Asner

———•———

Example is not the main thing in influencing others. It is the only thing.

—Albert Schweitzer

———•———

SCHOOL BOARDS

In the first place God made idiots. That was for practice. Then he made school boards.

—Mark Twain

Elected local school boards are unique to the U.S. and Canada. They limit standard-setting.

—Dr. Lester Thurow, MIT

SCHOOL BUS DRIVERS

The man who steps into a cage with a dozen lions impresses everybody except the school bus driver.

—from Farm Journal

SCHOOL SYSTEMS

There are only two places in the world where time takes precedence over the job to be done: school and prison.
—William Glasser

———•———

A school system without parents as its foundation is just like a bucket with a hole in it.
—Jesse Jackson

———•———

SCIENCE

Science is organized curiosity.
—Anonymous

———•———

Science is a little like the air you breathe—it is everywhere.
—Dwight D. Eisenhower

———•———

Science is facts; just as houses are made of stone, so is science made of facts; but a pile of stones is not a house and a collection of facts is not necessarily science.
—Henri Poincare

———•———

SEGREGATION

*Segregation is the offspring of an illicit
intercourse between injustice and immorality.*

—Martin Luther King, Jr.

———•———

*Busing is an artificial and
inadequate instrument of change.*

—Reuben Askey

———•———

SELF-ESTEEM

*Quien no sabe lo que vale no vale nada. (He who does not
know how much he is worth is worth nothing.)*

—Spanish Proverb

———•———

*I often dream about the day when every single youth in
this world will be able to lift their heads way, way,
way up high and say, "I believe in myself."*

—Laura Garcia, 17

———•———

The most widespread disease in the world is the inferiority complex.

—Stanley Sill

—•—

The current stairway to heaven is lined with celery sticks. Everyone wants to be Born Again—3 sizes smaller.

—Ellen Goodman

—•—

You're stronger than you seem; Braver than you believe; And smarter than you think you are.

—Christopher Robin
in Winnie the Pooh

—•—

You can't outperform your own image.

—Earnie Larson

—•—

SERVICE

Service is the rent we pay for living. It is the very purpose of life and not something you do in your spare time.

—Marian Wright Edelman,
The Measure of Our Success

—•—

SEX EDUCATION

Lord give me chastity—but not yet.

—Saint Augustine

*No matter where you hide your sex magazines,
your teenager will find them.*

—Bruce Lansky

If you can't be chaste, be cautious.

—Spanish Proverb

*We all worry about the population,
but we don't worry about it at the right time.*

—Arthur Hoppe

*We need to make a world in which fewer children are born,
and in which we take better care of them.*

—Dr. George Wald

The command to be fruitful and multiply
(was) promulgated . . . when the population of the world
consisted of two persons.
—Dean William R. Inge

———•———

Contraceptives should be used on every conceivable occasion.
—Spike Milligan

———•———

Sex is one of the three best things we have.
I don't know what the other two are.
—Helen Gurley Brown

———•———

If you aren't going all the way, why go at all?
—Joe Namath

———•———

Kids in the back seat cause accidents;
accidents in the backseat cause kids.
—Anonymous

———•———

In sexual intercourse, it's quality, not quantity, that counts.
—Dr. David Reuben

———•———

My town was so small that our school taught Driver's Ed. And Sex Ed. In the same car.

—Mary Sue Terry

———————

Actually, there is no such thing as a homosexual person, any more than there is such a thing as a heterosexual person. The words are adjectives describing sexual acts, not people.

—Gore Vidal

———————

SHAKESPEARE

It's rare that Shakespeare hasn't said something better about anything than almost anyone.

—Samuel Schuman, Chancellor,
University of Minnesota-Morris

———————

We've heard that a million monkeys at a million keyboards could produce the works of Shakespeare. Now, thanks to the Internet, we know this is not true.

—Making the rounds of the Internet

———————

SILENCE

God is a friend of silence.
—Mother Teresa

———•———

*Son, in this job you will have millions of opportunities
to keep your mouth shut. Take advantage of them all.*
—Dewey Knight

———•———

SIMPLICITY

You can learn from monks and hermits without being one.

Life is for living, not scheduling.
—Linus Mundy

———•———

*A visiting businessman standing on the pier of a small Mexican village watched a small boat and a single fisherman dock.
In the boat were a few tuna. The man
asked how long it took for the catch.*

"Not long," said the fisherman.

When the executive asked why he didn't stay to catch more,
the fisherman said he had enough to last a few days.

"But what do you do with the rest of your time?" the man asked.

"I sleep late, play with my kids, take siesta with my wife and then
stroll into the village to sing and play guitar with my amigos."

The dismayed businessman then offered to help the fisherman's
business grow by advising him to buy another boat. Then a
fleet. Later, he could open his own cannery. The fisherman
could then move to New York, issue an IPO. Of course, this
would all take 15-20 years of hard work. But it would be
worthwhile because the fisherman would then be rich.

"Then what?" wondered the fisherman.

"Why, you could retire, move to a small village, sleep late,
play with your kids, take siesta with your wife and stroll into
the village where you could sing and play guitar
with your amigos," said the executive.

—Anonymous from the Internet

———

For a child, doing nothing doesn't mean being inactive,
it means doing something that doesn't have a name.

There is nothing we can't do—
except, of course, doing nothing.

—Veronique Vienne

SMOKING

Tobacco was surely designed to poison and destroy mankind.

—Philip Frenean

I'm glad I don't have to explain to a man from Mars
why each day I set fire to dozens of little pieces of paper,
and then put them in my mouth.

—Mignon McLaughlin

Some things are better eschewed
than chewed. Tobacco is one of them.

—George Dennison Prentice

It is now proved beyond doubt that smoking is
one of the leading causes of statistics.

—Fletcher Knebel

SOCIAL LIFE

The social ramble ain't restful.

—Satchel Paige

———•———

SPACE

*I would be very ashamed of my civilization if we did not try
to find out if there is life in outer space.*

—Carl Sagan

———•———

*Someday, I would like to stand on the moon, look down
through a quarter of a million miles of space and say,
"There certainly is a beautiful earth out tonight."*

—Lt. Col. William Rankin

———•———

*The universe is not hostile, nor yet is it friendly.
It is simply indifferent.*

—John C. Holmes

———•———

SPORTS

It's kind of hard to rally 'round a math class.
—Paul "Bear" Bryant

* * *

One man practicing sportsmanship is far better than a hundred teaching it.
—Knute Rockne

* * *

Sports do not build character. They reveal it.
—Heywood Brown

* * *

I hate all sports as rabidly as a person who likes sports hates common sense.
—H. L. Mencken

* * *

Sports allow grown men to feel.
—Gail Sheehy

* * *

Winning is not everything—but making the effort to win is.
—Vince Lombardi

* * *

STANDARDS

*Franklin: Have you ever thought, Headmaster, that your
standards might perhaps be a little out-of-date?*

*Headmaster: Of course, they're out-of-date.
Standards are always out of date.
That's what makes them standards.*
—from the play Forty Years On
by Alan Bennett

You always do people a disservice by lowering the standard.
—Lou Holtz

To get better results, just raise the bar.
—Larry Bell

Consulting parents is not the way to set standards.
—Dr. Lester Thurow, MIT

STATISTICS

*T*here are three kinds of lies: lies, damned lies, and statistics.
—Benjamin Disraeli

———•———

*S*tatistics are like a bikini: What they reveal is suggestive,
but what they conceal is vital.
—Aaron Levenstein

———•———

*S*tatistics are for losers.
—Scotty Brown

———•———

SUCCESS

*S*urrounding yourself with dwarfs does not make you a giant.
—Yiddish folk saying

———•———

*U*ntil you're ready to look foolish,
you'll never have the possibility of being great.
—Cher

———•———

To be great is to be equal to the task.

—Sumo wrestler's slogan

———•———

My formula for success? Rise early, work late, strike oil.

—Jean Paul Getty

———•———

Definition of a Successful Life:
To laugh often and much;
to win the respect of intelligent people
and the affection of children;
to earn the appreciation of honest critics
and endure the betrayal of false friends;
to appreciate beauty, to find the best in others;
to leave the world a bit better,
whether by a healthy child,
a garden path or a redeemed social condition;
to know even one life has breathed easier
because you have lived.

—Ralph Waldo Emerson

———•———

Key to success: Find a niche—and then scratch it.

—Laurie Beth Jones

———•———

If A equals success, then the formula is A = X + Y + Z.
X is work. Y is play. Z is keep your mouth shut.

—Albert Einstein

———•———

Another secret to success is to work like a dog.

—Gen. Colin Powell

———•———

If you're a CEO by age 40, but your kids don't
want to talk to you, you're not a success.

—Christopher Reeve

———•———

If at first you do succeed, try to hide your astonishment.

—Henry Banks

———•———

A successful executive is one who can delegate
all the responsibilities, shift all the blame
and appropriate all the credit.

—"Wit & Humor,"
Supervision *magazine*

———•———

If at first you do succeed, try something harder.

—Ann Landers

———•———

Eighty percent of success is showing up.
—Woody Allen

⸺•⸺

Success is never final; failure is never fatal.
—Bob Dole

⸺•⸺

Nothing is as vulnerable as entrenched success.
—Dr. Jim Benson

⸺•⸺

Success is only failure in embryo.
—Rupert Everett

⸺•⸺

Success is one thing you'll never be forgiven for.
—Kathie Lee Gifford

⸺•⸺

SUICIDE

*Your most important act every day is
to decide not to commit suicide.*
—Frank McCourt

⸺•⸺

*S*uicide is not a remedy.

—James A. Garfield

———•———

*T*here is no refuge from confession but suicide;
and suicide is confession.   .

—Daniel Webster

———•———

I have never read a suicide note that I
would want to have written.

—Edwin Schneidman,
suicide expert

———•———

SUPPORT

*E*ither back us or sack us.

—James Gallaghan

———•———

*W*hat I want is men who will support me
when I am in the wrong.

—Lord Melbourne

———•———

T

TATTOOS

*Tattoos outlive 90% of the relationships
that inspire them. Think before you ink.*

—Anonymous

——•——

*With an increase in tattoos,
there's an increase in buyers' remorse.*

—Dr. Richard Tholen,
plastic surgeon

——•——

*It's hard to avoid a personal judgment
when a tattoo is visible.*

—Kristen Accipiter

——•——

*Why not tattoo? Kids love 'em. But parents can point out
that they're one form of foolery that won't fade away.*

—Amy Dickinson,
Time *magazine*

——•——

If you're willing to take tattoos seriously . . .
you'll find the right tattoo and the right place to put it.
Later in life . . . there will be no regrets.

—Chris Pfouts,
Editor, Tattoo *magazine*

———•———

TAXES

The art of taxation consists in so plucking the goose
as to get the most feathers with the least hissing.

—Jean Baptist Colbert

———•———

If Patrick Henry thought that taxation without representation
was bad, he should see how bad it is with representation.

—*from* The Old Farmers' Almanac

———•———

Collecting more taxes than is
absolutely necessary is legalized robbery.

—Calvin Coolidge

———•———

I'm proud to be paying taxes in the United States.
The only thing is—I could be just as happy
for half the money.

—Arthur Godfrey

———•———

Why does a slight tax increase cost you two hundred dollars and a substantial tax cut save you thirty cents?
—Peg Bracken

TEACHING

We, the unwilling, led by the unqualified, have been doing the unbelievable for so long for so little, we now attempt the impossible with nothing.
—Teacher's Creed,
(source unknown)

Teaching is the real world—it's like making love standing up in a hammock—you need balance, grace and a hell-of-a-lot of perseverance.
—Hanoch McCarty

" Come to the edge," he said.
They said, "We are afraid."
"Come to the edge," he said.
They came.
He pushed them.
And they flew.
—Guillaume Apollinaire

Questioner: If I became a great teacher, who would ever know?

Response: You, your students and God. Not a bad audience.
—*from the movie* A Man for All Seasons

———•———

Let me see if I have this right. You want me to go into that room with all those kids and fill their every waking moment with a love of learning. Not only that, but I am also to instill a sense of pride in their ethnicity, modify disruptive behavior, and observe them for signs of abuse.

I am to fight the war on drugs and sexually transmitted diseases, check their back packs for guns and knives and raise their self esteem. I am to teach them patriotism, good citizenship, sportsmanship and fair play; how to balance a checkbook, and how to apply for a job. . . .

I am to do all this with a piece of chalk, a bulletin board and a few books (some of which I may have to purchase myself), and for doing this, I am to be paid a starting salary that, in some states, qualifies me for food stamps.

Is that all?
—Anonymous letter to Ann Landers
(syndicated column)

———•———

*Why in the world are salaries higher for administrators
when the basic mission is teaching?*
—Jerry Brown,
former Governor of California

———•———

*Too often children are given answers to remember
rather than problems to solve.*
—Robert Lewin

———•———

A good teacher is better than a barrel full of books.
—Chinese Proverb

———•———

*Teachers are messengers from
the past and an escort to the future.*
—Albert Einstein

———•———

Repetition is the mother of skill.
—Anonymous

———•———

*They do everything but leap tall buildings for their students.
Their super hearing detects questions from teenagers before
they're even asked. They pluck kids from short attention spans
and awe them with new discoveries. Their keen vision
sees potential when others can't.*

While it may be hard to recognize teachers on the street,
it's easy to recognize the results of their work in the classroom.
—Ad for Education Minnesota
(affiliate of AFT & NEA)

---

*S*poon feeding in the long run teaches us
nothing but the shape of the spoon.
—E. M. Forster

---

*A*ll too often we are giving our young people cut flowers
when we should be teaching them to grow their own plants.
—John Gardner

---

*A*lways use plain talk with parents. They need help
and direction, not mumbo jumbo.
—from 501 Tips for Teachers

A wow in the classroom means something is happening.
—Frank McCourt

A call to all teachers—
"Somebody needs you. America needs you."
—Larry Bell

To teach is to learn.

—Japanese Proverb

———————

Teaching is the greatest act of optimism.

—Colleen Wilcox

———————

TECHNOLOGY

Technology is a great, growling engine of change.

—Dr. Jim Benson

———————

Those who live by electronics die by electronics.

—Kurt Vonnegut

———————

Technology . . . the knack of so arranging the world that we don't have to experience it.

—Max Frisch

———————

In 5-10 years, we'll have the technology to close every store in the world.

—Dr. Lester Thurow, MIT

———————

*It's the FUD factor—fear, uncertainty and doubt—
and it applies to any new technology.*
—Ben Alberti

*Somewhere between Sputnik and the computer,
morality got lost.*
—Thomas Lickana

*With our e-mail boxes and our faxes and phone machines
always "on," we have invaded our own solitude.*
—Gail Sheehy

*Technological progress has merely provided us with
more efficient means of going backwards.*
—Aldous Huxley

All technology should be assumed guilty until proven innocent.
—David Brower

*Technology is not an add-on item in our schools.
Students use computers as they use
books, pencils and paste.*
—St. Louis Park (MN) School News

TEENAGERS

*Having taught teens . . . I know with some certainty
that to them, everything is embarrassing.*

—Renee Rosenblum-Lowden

———•———

Most adolescents underestimate their own magnificence.

—Anonymous

———•———

*In the end all teenagers want to be cared for and
paid attention to. They just go about getting
love and attention in different ways.*

—Emily Foster,
high school senior

———•———

Normal adolescence is sometimes very abnormal.

—Leigh Abrahamson,
school social worker

———•———

*Puberty is the period when students stop asking questions
and begin to question answers.*

—Anonymous

———•———

*T*eenagers are people who express a burning desire
to be different by dressing exactly alike.

—Anonymous

———•———

TELEVISION

I find television very educational. Every time someone
turns it on, I go in the other room and read a book.

—Groucho Marx

———•———

*W*hen television is bad, nothing is worse.

—Newton Norman Minow

———•———

*T*V rots the senses in the head!
It kills the imagination dead!
It clogs and clutters up the mind!
It makes a child so dull and blind,
He can no longer understand a fantasy,
A fairy land!
His brain becomes as soft as cheese!
His powers of thinking rust and freeze!

—Ronald Dahl
(*from* Charlie & The Chocolate Factory)

———•———

TV is leading children down a moral sewer.
—Steve Allen

———◆———

The vast wasteland of TV is not interested in producing a better mousetrap but in producing a worse mouse.
—Laurence Coughlin

———◆———

We are drowning our youngsters in violence, cynicism and sadism piped into the living room and even the nursery.
—Marian Wright Edelman

———◆———

TV—chewing gum for the mind.
—Frank Lloyd Wright

———◆———

Men don't want to know what's on TV.
They want to know what else is on TV.
—Zig Ziglar

———◆———

[Television] a medium, so called because it is neither rare nor well done.
—Ernie Kovacs,
Comedian

———◆———

The sky is better than television sometimes.
—Peg Wheary

———◆———

TEMPTATION

The biggest human temptation is . . . to settle for too little.
—Thomas Merton

———

TESTING

Examinations are formidable even to the best prepared,
for the greatest fool may ask more
than the wisest man can answer.
—Charles Caleb Colton

———

You can't fatten the cattle by weighing them.
You have to feed them.
—Dr. Paul D. Houston

———

If you can't measure it, you can't manage it.
—Ed Lisoki

———

What gets measured, gets done.
—Tom Peters

———

Not everything that counts can be counted.

—Anonymous

———•———

THINKING

Most people would die sooner than think. Most do.

—Bertrand Russell

———•———

Nothing pains some people more than having to think.

—Martin Luther King, Jr.

———•———

You should never think everything I'm thinking
'cause then only one of us is thinking.

—Ice-T (rapper)

———•———

Change your thoughts and you change your world.

—Norman Vincent Peale

———•———

TIME

I must govern the clock, not be governed by it.

—Golda Meir

———•———

You never know how soon it will be too late.

—Ralph Waldo Emerson

———•———

There is time for work. And time for love.
That leaves no other time.

—Coco Chanel

———•———

Time is God's way of keeping everything
from happening at once.

—Anonymous

———•———

Half our life is spent trying to find something to do with
the time we have rushed through trying to save.

—Will Rogers

———•———

Time is a circus always picking up and moving on.

—Ben Hecht

———•———

Time is the stream I go a-fishing in.

—Henry David Thoreau

———•———

U

UNIONS

*Unionism seldom, if ever, uses such power as it has to insure
better work, almost always it devotes a large part of
that power to safeguard bad work.*

—H. L. Mencken

———•———

*With all their faults, trade unions have done more for
humanity than any other organization
of men that ever existed.*

—Clarence Darrow

———•———

VIOLENCE

What makes boys violent? We do.
—William Pollack

—•—

Students are more likely to be killed
in their home than in school.
—Irwin Hyman, president,
American Academy of School Psychologists

—•—

You can build a fortress, but if someone wants to
do something violent, he'll find a way.
You have to change what's inside.
—Nicole Signorette,
16-year-old student

—•—

Schools need "mental detectors," not metal detectors.
—Anonymous psychologist

—•—

We've all been blessed with God-given talents. Mine just happens to be beating people up.
—Sugar Ray Leonard

———

You know I hate fighting. If I knew how to make a living some other way, I would.
—Muhammad Ali

———

Combat is dangerous. It tends to interrupt your breathing process.
—Joe Foss,
World War II hero

———

You cannot shake hands with a clenched fist.
—Indira Gandhi

———

Violence is counterproductive. It is a dangerous instrument and can destroy those who wield it.
—John Gardner

———

Today violence is the rhetoric of the period.
—José y Ortega Gasset

VIRTUE

*We have come to a place, a time when
virtue is no longer a virtue.*
—Maya Angelou

Do good and leave behind a monument of virtue.
—*from* Wisdom of the Plain Folk

VISION

Vision without resources is hallucination.
—Mark Yudof, President,
University of Minnesota

*Questioner: Is losing your eyesight the worst thing
that can happen to someone?*

Helen Keller: No, losing your vision is.
—Source unknown

Vision without action is merely a dream.
—Joel Barker, futurist

Vision is seeing the invisible.
> —Jonathan Swift

———◆———

Perseverance is essential—
You don't persevere without a vision.
> —Dr. Lester Thurow, MIT

———◆———

Without a vision the people will perish.
> —King Solomon

———◆———

VOLUNTEERS

Volunteers are like Ford, they have better ideas.
Volunteers are like Coke, they are the real thing.
Volunteers are like Pan Am, they make the going great.
Volunteers are like Pepsi, they've got a lot to give.
Volunteers are like Dial Soap, they care more.
Volunteers are like VO-5 hairspray,
their goodness holds in all weather.
Volunteers are like Hallmark Cards,
they care enough to give their very best.
Volunteers are like Standard Oil,
you expect more and you get it.

Volunteers are like Frosted Flakes,
they're GRRRRRREAT!

—Courtesy of
55 Alive Mature Driving

———•———

VOTING

Do you ever get the feeling that the only reason we
have elections is to find out if the polls are right?

—Robert Orben

———•———

The idea that you can merchandise candidates for
high office like breakfast cereal—that you can gather votes
like box tops—is, I think, the ultimate indignity
of the democratic process.

—Adlai Stevenson

———•———

In years divisible by two we expect the
truth to be trashed and decency to be mugged.

—George F. Will

———•———

Ballots are the rightful and peaceful successors to bullets.

—Abraham Lincoln

———•———

VOUCHERS

*And one thing about school choice is that it offers
immediate opportunities to children who are in
bad schools to go to good schools—today.*

—Clint Bolick

*Vouchers would move tax funded American education
away from . . . democratic control, pluralism and accountability
toward a maze of multiple school systems often typified by
selective discrimination . . . not responsible or
accountable to the taxpaying public.*

—Albert Menendez
& John Swomley

WOMAN

Woman was God's second mistake.
—Friedrich Nietzsche

God made man and then said,
"I can do better than that,"—and made woman.
—Adele St. Johns

Women's place is in the House . . . and in the Senate.
—Gloria Schaffer

WORDS

Syllables govern the world.
—John Selden

Words are, of course, the most powerful drug used by mankind.
—Rudyard Kipling

———•———

When I use a word, it means just what I choose it to mean.
—Lewis Carroll

———•———

WORK

The world is full of people—some willing to work, the rest willing to let them.
—Robert Frost

———•———

We work to live, not live to work.
—Carl Holmstrom

———•———

Everyone should learn the meaning of that famous little four-letter word—work.
—Bob Bush,
Congressional Medal of Honor recipient

———•———

Work chooses the man.
—Sophy Burnham

———•———

*E*very calling is great when it's greatly pursued.

—*Anonymous*

———•———

*C*hoose a job you love and you will
never have to work a day in your life.

—*Confucius*

———•———

*A*lways take a job that is too big for you.

—Harry Emerson Fosdick

———•———

*P*eople should tell their children
what life is about—it's about work.

—Lauren Bacall

———•———

*W*e work to become, not to acquire.

—*Elbert Hubbard*

———•———

*A*ll jobs are temporary—always were and always will be—
but there will always be work.

—Anonymous

———•———

WORRY

*We are, perhaps, uniquely among the earth's creatures,
the worrying animal.*

—Lewis Thomas

———•———

*Worry a little every day, and in a lifetime you will
lose a couple of years. . . . Worry never fixes anything.*

—Mary Welsh Hemingway

———•———

*When I look back on all these worries, I remember the story
of an old man who said on his deathbed that he had a lot of
troubles in his life, most of which never happened.*

—Winston Churchill

———•———

WRITING

I love being a writer. What I can't stand is the paperwork.

—Peter De Vries

———•———

*If I had to give young writers advice, I'd say don't listen to
writers talking about writing.*

—Lillian Hellman

———•———

Write to express, not to impress.

—Bob Bly

I see but one rule: to be clear.

—Stendahl

No manuscript is ever finished, only abandoned.

—Ann Regan

---

*It wasn't by accident that the
Gettysburg Address was so short.*

—Ernest Hemingway

---

*Writing is easy. All you do is sit staring at the blank sheet
of paper until drops of blood form on your forehead.*

—Red Smith

YOUTH

Youth is a disease from which we all recover.
—Dorothy Fuldheim

⬥

Youth is the trustee of posterity.
—Disraeli

⬥

Youth is an attitude, not an age.
—Anonymous

⬥

ZERO TOLERANCE

I must be cruel to be kind.
—Shakespeare

⬥

*K*ids *need to know there are consequences to illegal acts.*
—Jim Pasco,
Police Union leader

———————

*W*e've *got kids getting kicked out of school
for saying bang-bang to each other.*
—Vincent Schiraidi

———————

A vocal *minority . . . has gone overboard on safety to
demand zero tolerance. Unfortunately, school administrators
are left with virtually no discretion.*
—Erick Kaardal

———————

ZOO

*W*hen *I was a kid I said to my father one afternoon,
"Daddy, will you take me to the zoo?" He answered,
"If the zoo wants you, let them come and get you."*
—Jerry Lewis

———————

OTHER RESOURCES YOU SHOULD KNOW ABOUT

*Y*ou never know where or when you will find just the right thought wrapped in just the right phrase. Perfect quotes don't flock together. You have to find them one by one.

If you want to continue your quest for notable quotables, check out the diverse and unusual sources below (each is a one-of-a-kind collection):

ben Shea, Noah. (2000). *What every principal would like to say . . . And what to say next time.* Thousand Oaks, CA: Corwin.

Leahy, Robert. (1997). *Wisdom of the plain folk.* New York: Penquin Books.

Mickenerg, Risa. (1996). *Taxi driver wisdom.* San Francisco: Chronicle Books.

Phillips, Larry W. (1984). *Ernest Hemingway on writing.* New York: Simon & Schuster.

Shanahan, John M. (1959). *The most brilliant thoughts of all time (in two lines or less).* New York: Cliff Street Books.

Warner, Carolyn. (1992). *Treasury of woman's quotations.* Englewood Cliffs, NJ: Prentice Hall.